To Chris
with love,

Betty

READY

AIM

RETIRE

John A. Kessler

∞INFINITY
PUBLISHING

ISBN 0-7414-6634-1

Printed in the United States of America

Published June 2011

INFINITY PUBLISHING
1094 New DeHaven Street, Suite 100
West Conshohocken, PA 19428-2713
Toll-free (877) BUY BOOK
Local Phone (610) 941-9999
Fax (610) 941-9959
Info@buybooksontheweb.com
www.buybooksontheweb.com

Dedication

During frustrating moments and endless delays, I always got back on track through the support and encouragement of my loving wife Marion.

"My task which I am trying to achieve is by the power of the written word. To make you hear, to make you feel - it is, before all, to make you see. That and no more, and it is everything."

Joseph Conrad
1857-1924

TABLE OF CONTENTS

INTRODUCTION

We have all heard of those Life Altering events, which may cause stress, illness and a variety of other issues. These events generally include Marriage, Divorce, Birth of Child, Death in Family, Buying a New Home and Loss of a Job.

Rarely mentioned but an equally important event in our lives is Retirement! While these Life Altering events define our ongoing life, retirement defines the final stage of our life.

In the following pages, I have attempted to put together a variety of subjects that will stimulate your thought process and give you much to consider as you plan for your retirement and the years that follow. Even if you have already retired you may find this material helpful. This is not a manual of how to invest your money, locate a home or find a retirement job, but rather it is designed to make you think seriously about all of the components that will go into creating a happy retirement.

After many years in a Human Resources career during which I counseled and advised numerous employees as they approached their retirement, I marvel at the lack of interest displayed by most people about this subject. Likewise, I find the same to be true with relatives and friends. Generally, excuses given for not discussing retirement fall into several categories such as: I am too young to worry about that now, I am too busy with life and its problems now, and the classic, I have plenty of time to worry about that later!

I have vivid memories of employees always telling me how many years, months and days they had until retirement and yet never once adding any discussion as to how they were going to handle it.

Ignoring the subject has led to many sad events that could have been avoided with just a little forethought. I will relate just a few of them to set the stage for this writing.

In my last position when an employee announced they were planning to retire, we had a practice of preparing and submitting their retirement papers for an estimate of their benefits. When their plan was approved we would sit down with the employee, go over the details and ultimately personally present their first retirement check. I remember one employee looking at the check and almost in a panic mode she said, "I can't possibly get by on this amount of money, is this all there is"?

Then there was the wife of a retired employee who came to see me when her husband passed away and said she did not receive any Life Insurance or Pension benefit. I sadly had to explain to her that her late husband had failed to change his beneficiary designation and his first wife had received all of the benefits as the Beneficiary.

Another employee retired and when she left said, "I couldn't wait for this day to get out of here; I'm going to really enjoy myself". It was not long after that she stopped back in to see me and asked if she could come back to work as she was bored and had nothing to do with herself.

Another employee had long suffered with a terminal illness and I had counseled her to take a certain course of action that would have insured some death benefits to her needy children. She procrastinated and kept saying she still had time to work things out. Guess what, she did not have the time left and the children lost out.

Recently I heard a story about an older woman who went to a Tax Preparer to have income taxes completed. She had very little in the way of documentation to present as she explained that her Husband who always did this type of thing was seriously ill in the hospital and she had no idea where anything was.

I relate these stories to show how lack of proper planning and attention to retirement can often have dire consequences, and to make you aware of just how critical it is that everyone think well ahead and be prepared for that important day when retirement turns from dream to reality.

Consider the following facts about older Americans, which were compiled by the Administration on Aging of the U.S. Department of Health & Human Services.

1. One in eight of the population is an older American.

2. The number of people 65 and older on July 1. 2009 was 39.6million or 13% of the total population. By 2050, that number will grow to 20% of the population.

3. Persons reaching age 65 have a life expectancy of an additional 18.6 years.

4. Women far outlive men by a ratio of about three to one.

5. The number of older Americans reaching 100 jumped 14.7% between 1990 and 2008.

6. The number of Americans reaching 65 and over will increase by 15% in 2010 and by 2020 will increase an additional 36%.

7. Social Security constituted 90% of the income received by 35% of all Social Security beneficiaries.

This is important information for all of us to know and understand. The significance of it shows that more and more older Americans will be relying on a smaller pool of government money and that they will increasingly be drawing on it and their own personal savings over a longer life span. Of particular note is the fact that women continue to outpace men in the longevity race and therefore women must be extra cautious in assessing their future. We must all remember that these increasing numbers will cause additional strain on services required by older Americans particularly in the Health Care field. Yes, it is a different world out there and it is critical that all of us plan accordingly for our Retirement years.

In the pages that follow, I will cover a variety of subjects, which will gently take you through the steps that should be considered in order for you to have a happy and carefree retirement. You may believe that you are well prepared but I suspect you will find a number of things that could surprise you and at the very least will give you food for thought.

Please do not think that Retirement Planning is for the "old folks" because the reality is that you should have started this process many years before you actually are ready to retire. My intention in putting this book together is to alert a wide audience ranging from those just starting out to those who are in the middle years and finally to those reaching retirement and beyond.

I am afraid that while everyone looks forward to the so-called "Golden Years", we find that in real life, retirement is probably much closer to various shades of grey!

Carefully consider what you read in the following pages and hopefully these thoughts and observations will lead you into the twilight of your life in a more gentle and orderly fashion.

HAVE A HAPPY RETIREMENT!

"Preparation for old age should begin no later than one's teens. A life which is empty of purpose until 65 will not suddenly become filled on retirement."

Arthur E. Morgan

1878-1975

PLANNING

We all remember when our Grandparents or Mom and Dad retired. There was probably a luncheon where they worked and after that, life went on pretty much the way it always had. Mom still got up early, fixed breakfast and proceeded to clean the house, do laundry, etc. Dad got up, ate breakfast and started puttering around the yard or the house. Same with the Grandparents. Yes, life did seem and was in fact a little more simple.

I am certain that we all know people who seemed to have their retirement life well sorted out and planned. These folks simply picked up and moved South or West. They had in pre-retirement years identified that special place where they wanted to be. There was no question as to where or how they were going to live. They had also made an early decision to leave family and friends and establish a new life in a new environment.

However, today the dream of a warm Southern or Western destination has become less certain because of the Real Estate market or even more so because of family concerns. What could some of these concerns be? For starters, consider that in recent years growing numbers of our children have not been striking out on their own as much as we did, but in fact are returning home to live with their parents. This is due largely to the lack of jobs and the corresponding poor condition of their finances. Additionally, we now see many more parents and grandparents assuming responsibility as caregivers for children and grandchildren. There is also a growing trend for families to pool their resources and move in together.

However, today we all face a dramatically changed world, which requires a completely different approach to our retirement life. Some of the biggest and most critical things that have changed for most of us are the state of our finances. Who would have ever thought that retirement savings would disappear or shrink? As for pensions, we all thought they were virtually sacred yet how many plans have been discontinued or gone away due to funding issues?

Confusing the Retirement subject even further is the now critical condition of our Social Security program which most people never even concerned themselves with. It was always taken for granted that "IT" would be there. However, even as you read this, there are growing signs that Social Security as we know it will be significantly changed in the coming years. An extremely disturbing development has been the lack of a benefit increase for the past two years, and it appears likely that increased costs in the Medicare insurance portion of Social Security may erase any benefit increase in 2011.

Don't you wish now that you had taken the time and made the effort to seriously consider and plan for your Retirement? In addition, do not make the mistake that because you had a few conversations with your spouse and or your children that this will suffice for a well thought out plan for the rest of your life.

Remember, you have worked hard and deserve the opportunity to enjoy the Retirement years without constantly looking over your shoulder and wondering what is going to sneak up on you and make what should be a happy and troublesome time.

I believe that your Retirement Plan should be a well thought out document that outlines virtually every aspect of your life as it relates to Retirement. Please remember that life after work is somewhat different from the fully charged active life you had with work, children and maintaining a large home. You may think that nothing changes but believe me you will soon be faced with a completely different set of life changes and challenges.

Your planning ideally should have started many years before Retirement actually knocked on your door. However, do not fret if you still have not faced this issue because you can still put together a plan.

Chances are that you may feel somewhat overwhelmed with this task but you can do it! An important thing to remember is that you do not have to take on this task by yourself. Call in the troops! These being your children, your employee representative, a financial advisor, etc.

While your first inclination may to keep this matter private, you will be well served to get some advice from those around you in whom you have some trust and confidence. It would also be very worthwhile to have conversations with others you know whom have already retired. The insight of others can be a powerful tool to aid you in this important matter.

Using some of these resources will expand the scope of your planning and expose you to many ideas and options, which may not have occurred to you. I know that we all believe that involving others may be intrusive, and of course, we all think that much of this subject is nobody's business, but you can reap great benefits from the collaboration of others.

I know! Right about here you may be thinking, I know exactly what I am going to do when I retire. I will be staying right where I am, playing golf, going out to eat, visiting the kids, taking trips etc... I hear you and maybe some or all of that may be true but to coin that old saying we all hear," LIFE COMES AT YOU FAST!" In an instant, everything we had planned for changes and our life takes us in a direction other than the one we planned.

I often chuckle to myself when I see those ads, which display a Retiree gazing at the sunset while drinking wine on the patio, or even better, the older couple being ushered into the private jet for a trip to who knows where. I certainly do not begrudge the few who do manage these sorts of events but it just is not reality. They may have achieved this level of retirement as the result of good planning or an abundance of money.

Think for a moment of your own situation, or that of others you know. You will probably conclude that there is somewhat of a gap between what you see in the ads and what reality is. My sincere message here is that planning can alter your retirement years and help you avoid the pitfalls fallen on so many others.

Will planning solve all of your problems? Quite honestly it will not! However, it will prepare you for a more relaxed and enjoyable time and more importantly, alert you to and help guide you through those times and areas which may be troublesome.

The stark reality of retirement is that it unavoidably leads you to questions in your life for which you are unprepared.

What do I do when a spouse passes before I do?

Where am I going to live?

When do we give up the second car?

When do I stop driving?

Do I need some personal assistance?

How will I take care of household chores if I become ill?

How am I going to handle my personal finances?

There are, to be sure, many more questions that you will be faced with but these are a few of the common ones, which you will eventually have to face.

Therefore, you see, planning involves much more than just setting a date when you will stop working. As we continue in later chapters, you will see in more detail the depth of the many issues, which you should address.

It is never too late to plan and I hope you will take time to consider making your own personal Retirement Plan.

"The question isn't at what age I want to retire, it's at what income. "

George Foreman

1949

FINANCE

This subject will be one of your most important considerations. I hope that you have at the very least made some effort to judge and project what your financial needs will be and more importantly, where the money will be coming from! You must be aware of a new phenomenon taking place with older people. They are living longer and therefore a new situation is arising where more people are faced with outliving their savings!

Here is another fact that should provide a wakeup call for everybody planning for his or her retirement. A study released by Wells Fargo & Co. in December of 2010 revealed that Middle-Class Americans think they need $300,000 to fund their retirement, but on average have only saved $20,000 toward that goal.

A more recent poll conducted in March 2011 by The Associated Press-LifeGoesStrong.com., indicates that 44% of Baby Boomers (Those born between 1946-1964) believe they will not have enough money to retire.

On the subject of how much you should have saved for retirement there is no definitive answer as to what that figure should be. You need to determine what standard of living you wish to maintain in retirement and by doing so you can start to plan and map out your own personal strategy in order to accomplish that goal. Always keep in mind that you can never save too much!

Perhaps one of the biggest shocks many retirees get is the fact that your living expense may not change from what you are spending in your working years. For sure, we will all be faced with increasing costs for Health Care as well as such things as entertainment and taxes. Many people fall victim to all of the hype that you will only need a fraction of your normal income to live on during retirement.

Could be true for some but think for a moment about yourself. How much will you be willing to change the way you live now should finances dictate a reduction in your standard of living?

Say you plan to stay in the home you have lived in for many years. Consider that all of the normal expense you have today may remain the same in retirement. The difference will be that you will be on a fixed income. Remember those two words," FIXED INCOME". That means no more raises at work, perhaps no increase in your Social Security as has happened in the 2010 and 2011 years. Another important fact to remember about Social Security is that it may only provide somewhere in the neighborhood of 40% of your pre-retirement income. In addition, if you are depending on investment money from a 401K or IRA you may be shocked to find that they have suffered substantial decreases in value during the economic slowdown.

I strongly recommend that you find and use a reliable source that you have confidence in to assist you in developing a financial plan. However, even before you do this you should be making some basic good decisions about your money and how you manage it.

The first and most important decision you can ever make regarding your finances is to develop a SAVING ATTITUDE. Start to think in terms of being thrifty and money smart. Think carefully about how you are spending your money and constantly look for ways to cut your spending. The SAVING ATTITUDE is one habit that will serve you well throughout your life and into your retirement years. A key element in the SAVING ATTITUDE strategy is to always pay yourself first. Each payday set aside whatever you decide is doable and put it into some type of saving account. No matter how small you start out, you will be pleasantly surprised when you see how it grows.

You should create a budget and learn to live within it. This is a simple thing to do and it will become a valuable tool for you to use in managing your finances. Many of us have sailed through life without bothering to keep track of expenses on a regular basis.

Believe me when I tell you that a written budget plan will keep you right on top of your expenses and give you some warning about impending problems. Especially as you get older and move into retirement you will be surprised just how valuable a budget will become to you.

While you are working, your company may have a 401K Plan. I cannot urge you strongly enough to join such a plan as it remains one of the last best investment decisions you can make. Most companies who have such a plan will either match or contribute a percentage of your match into the plan. Many people will say that I cannot put that money away as I need it each payday. The simple answer is, start slow, but start! As your situation improves, you can up your contribution. You must remember that the good old days of a company pension are all but gone and the 401K will be your pension fund. An important fact to remember here is that the old pension plans gave you a definite amount of money you could plan on whereas the 401K is a moving target subject to the whims of the economy. It is important that you seek some counsel to help you wisely direct your savings in such a plan!

An excellent savings opportunity for you to explore is the ROTH IRA. This permits you to invest pretax dollars while you are working and then enjoy tax free distribution upon Retirement.

Another saving method you might employ is to buy U. S Bonds through a payroll plan or go directly to your bank and purchase them. These are secure investments that will guarantee income for later in life.

Have you purchased Life Insurance? This should be a consideration for your long term planning. It is a way to pass on tax-free money to your children or other beneficiaries. It may also be a good strategy in terms of helping to cover inheritance taxes and other final expenses. Due to its cost this is something you should consider earlier rather than later as the ability to purchase insurance rises dramatically as you age.

If you project a shortfall in your retirement income then perhaps an Annuity would be right for you. This is a saving vehicle that can be set up to provide you with an income stream during retirement. Annuities come in many varieties and you should research them thoroughly before you decide on one.

One of the most common and popular investment methods is the Certificate of Deposit (CD). These have proven to be a safe and secure way to save money and in the past, they generated high rates of return. In recent years, they have fallen from favor by many because of the very low rate of return they have. However, they are very safe and secure and provide a safe haven for your money.

Now here is a blockbuster that most of us did not expect! We always felt comfortable in the fact that we would have substantial equity in our home. However, who would have foreseen the catastrophic blow to the Real Estate market? This was money we expected would help fund our retirement in many different ways. Quite the opposite has occurred as houses that can be sold are selling for substantially less than expected. Many people have planned for years to use the proceeds from what they thought would be a windfall to purchase the retirement home of their dreams. I hope that your dream will not turn out to be a bad nightmare! If you are lucky and planned well, maybe you were fortunate enough to have your house completely paid off and you will be in better financial shape. On this particular subject, you should be considering paying off your house as early as it is financially feasible to do so. This is something you will wish to discuss with an advisor.

In all of your financial planning, there is one essential and important thing you must do and that is to designate your BENEFICIARIES AND MAKE CERTAIN THESE ARE UP TO DATE!

You must remember that upon your passing all of your assets will pass to a designated Beneficiary. I have seen in many cases where an individual has failed to change a beneficiary after a marriage, remarriage, death, or other life event. In addition, you must be aware that because of Bank mergers, Investment House mergers, companies going out of business and other events, your beneficiary information may have been lost or misplaced.

I cannot stress enough the importance of keeping a current watch on this subject so that you and your survivors will not suffer later.

You will be well served to examine your Credit Card situation. You do not ever want to get into a pattern of overextending your credit. This will especially be a serious problem if you retire, depend on Credit Card spending to get by on, and then wake up to find that you have to go into savings to get out of debt.

Here is an idea for you to consider and one, which I have used and recommended to others. Hold a Financial meeting with your spouse at least on a quarterly schedule. It is extremely important that you both know exactly what is going on in your financial life. I understand that one or the other generally pays bills, does the banking and handles the savings. For whatever reason you have done this you should carefully consider the importance of each knowing what is going on! Think for a moment what happens when there is illness, death or any other type of event where one of you is suddenly thrust into the role of becoming the caretaker of the finances. How do you approach something so important when you might not have any idea what you have to do?

For example, have you ever written out checks to pay bills, do you know where everything is, how much is in the accounts, where they are or what might have to be done with investments? Remember that as you age your abilities age with you and one of you may not have the cognitive ability you enjoyed in your younger years. I cannot stress enough the importance of carrying on a shared responsibility for all of your financial decisions.

In your younger and middle years, you should investigate the feasibility of purchasing Long Term Care Insurance. Such a purchase may save you a lot of grief if the time ever comes when you need home assistance, nursing home or assisted living care. If you do consider such a purchase, examine the various types of plans that are available as they can offer a wide range of benefits for you to consider. Remember that if you decide to purchase Long Term Care Insurance at an older age, you will pay substantially higher premiums.

I mentioned earlier the subject of obtaining a Financial Advisor to assist you in setting up your Retirement plans and goals. This is a smart way to go and you can easily find good advisors with a little effort. I have found that Banks, Insurance Agencies, Insurance Companies, 401K Plan Administrators are generally good sources of financial advice. Depending on the level of advice you seek, the cost of such services can range from nothing up to a small percentage of your holdings.

There is one other area which I believe is worthy of serious attention. Unfortunately, the financial status of many older Americans has and will continue to suffer and as a result, they will struggle to just meet their basic needs. I urge anybody who finds himself or herself in this situation to seek out the many avenues of help that are available to them. These include, rent assistance, food assistance, energy assistance, tax abatement and medical assistance. The Federal Government, your State, County and Local authorities have many programs available to help you. You may also benefit from such programs as the Meal-on -Wheels, lunch programs at your Senior Center and programs administered by your Church. Please do not be shy or feel ashamed in any way to seek out the services that are available to you.

I cannot leave this section without mentioning Credit Cards. This little story about Credit Cards to start. I was recently in a Department store waiting for my wife to pick out some clothes. While she was busy, I wandered over by the check out register to wait. A young woman was purchasing a quantity of clothing while her Mother, a senior citizen, waited nearby. The daughter turned and asked her Mother for a credit card. To my amazement, the older woman rummaged in her purse and came out with two hands full of credit cards that were banded together in stacks of perhaps 10/12 in each group. As she fumbled through them, some fell and the daughter dutifully retrieved them. Two thoughts occurred to me at that point. The first was what a setting for disaster! Who knows how often that scene is repeated and how easy it would be for somebody to grab a card? Second thought was why would anybody carry and display that many credit cards? The potential for identity theft and other problems is just too great. Sound judgment would tell you that one, two or maybe three cards are more than enough in today's economy. You must be aware that the recent changes in the Credit Card laws have forced those companies to dramatically change the way they attach fees and interest charges to the cards. So, be aware of exactly what you have, how much it may be costing you and be certain you keep them secure.

On this matter of Financial Security, you should also consider keeping track of your Credit Rating. It is a simple way to watch for identity theft and possible misuse of your credit. Remember, under Federal Law you are entitled to a free Credit Report from each of the major credit agencies annually at no charge to you. Please use this to your advantage. The three Credit Reporting agencies that you will wish to check with are Trans Union, Experian and Equifax.

Another area that may yield seniors financial benefits is in the area of their Real Estate taxes. Many states, counties, cities and towns offer a variety of tax incentives you should investigate. These include tax reductions for seniors, Veterans, low income and disabled parties. You will wish to contact your local tax authority to obtain information relative to these programs.

One last comment about finances that many people do not wish to hear and that involves the children. We all love our children but do not make the critical mistake of being overly generous with the kids at the expense of diminishing your financial resources. No question that times are tough and we all have that natural urge to bail them out of every situation. However, remember you cannot predict what your needs will be due to any number of catastrophic events that might come upon you in a flash. You worked your entire life to insure a safe and comfortable retirement and you must avoid anything that jeopardizes that! Your Financial health will be important as you move into your Retirement years and if you have planned properly then this will be one less worry for you.

When preparing for retirement you will greatly rely on your Social Security benefits. Some points you will wish to consider in this regard are:

1. Get an estimate of what your benefit will be. You may do this by obtaining a "Request for Earnings and Benefits Estimate Statement" from the Social Security office. After you submit the form, you will receive your estimate and then can use this as a planning tool.

2. Consider your Social Security plans very carefully. You may not be aware of the fact that there are a number of options available to you as to how you may collect your benefit. Depending on your financial needs you may wish to delay your benefit which you may do up to the age of 70. At age 70, you would enjoy a higher benefit. Whatever you decide, carefully consider all of your options and seek advice from a trusted advisor, children or family member.

One final comment which I will refer to as my GOLDEN RULE! If you can plan your retirement finances so that your monthly income in retirement is adequate to meet your expenses, then you will be GOLDEN. If you can preserve and even grow your capital while living off the monthly income that you receive, then you will insure your financial stability and have available funds for those unexpected events that invariably pop up.

REMEMBER -PLAN YOUR FINANCES, MONITOR THEM AND SPEND THEM WISELY!

"He who has good health is young"

H. G. Bohn

1796-1884

HEALTH

Your health will be the single most important issue you must face as you near retirement. Again citing data released by the Administration on Aging, in 2008, 39.1% of non-institutional older persons assessed their health as excellent or very good. This is in comparison to 60.7% for all persons over 18. In addition, hospital stays for those over 65 averaged 5.5 days per patient, which was three times the comparable rate for persons of all ages. Obviously, the conclusion here is that as you age your health will probably decline in some fashion.

In 2008, older consumers averaged out-of-pocket health care expenditures of $4,605, an increase of 57% since 1998. This compares to the total population, which spent an average of $2976 in out-of-pocket expenses. Older Americans spent 12.5% of their total expenditures on health, which was more than twice the proportion spent by all consumers.

The questions everybody needs to address are; How are we going to pay for the care we will need and who will provide it? Again, the old conventional thinking was that we did not worry about such things; our Medicare and Medicaid were out there to take care of us. Additionally we would always have Family to step in whenever they were needed. However, we all know that times have changed significantly and the old thinking no longer applies.

There is no secret that the future of Medical Care has been a topic on the minds of virtually everybody in our country. It has become a complicated tangle of issues as the Government, the Medical Industry, the Pharmaceutical Industry, The Insurance Industry and multiple Private Interest groups debate the merits of their own perception of what quality Medical Care should be.

The real problem with all of these conflicting points of view is that the real beneficiaries of the issue, we the people, have had little meaningful input into the matter. In reality, our views have been largely ignored!

As far as the older population is concerned, there are several key points of which we all need to be aware. First it is no secret that the life expectancy of the older population has become longer as each year passes. The latest data issued by the Center for Disease Control and Prevention indicates the average life expectancy of Americans is now 78.2 years. For Males, the figure is 75.6 and for females, 80.5.This in itself means quite simply that we will need Medical Care for much longer than originally expected. This in turn presents the situation where significantly more money will be required to pay for a Health Delivery System. Increasingly, the burden of paying for HealthCare has been shifting to the consumer. As an employee, you most likely saw your share of paying for Medical benefits increase virtually every year. As a Retiree, you are also seeing changes in your Retiree Medical benefits, which range from increased cost sharing to outright elimination of these benefits.

As for Medicare and Medicaid, you are no doubt aware of the many changes currently under discussion concerning its funding.

Of necessity, due to these concerns, it will be in your best interest to explore alternative back up measures to insure you are adequately protected. These may include one or more of the following:

1. **Supplemental Medical Insurance** to pick up the gap between Medicare and what you may have to pay for Medical Care.

2. **Long Term Care Insurance** that would provide funds for Assisted Living, Nursing Home or Home Care.

3. **Dental Insurance** that will help cover Dental costs.

I am not suggesting that these types of additional coverage are for everybody as each person must examine their own situation and act accordingly. These programs are all very good to have but they do come with a cost attached. This is the point where you have to do some serious planning to determine what is best for you.

You can also make a significant contribution to your overall health by keeping up a personal exercise program. There are so many easy ways to accomplish this in today's world. I recognize that not everybody is physically the same and while some forms of exercise are easy for some, they are extremely difficult for others. The most important thing to remember is that exercise is mainly a state of mind. You can develop either by yourself, with your medical professional, a friend or family member, a good exercise plan.

A significant area of concern for seniors is the growing cost of Prescription medication. Although there is some coverage for these medications, many find themselves with expenses they are unable to meet. If you have such a problem, I urge you to contact the Pharmaceutical Company and determine if they can help you as many of them have programs to help. You may also wish to check into the drug plans offered by drug store chains and many retailers.

Walking can become a key ingredient of exercise for virtually anybody. It can be walking around the block, on a treadmill or in the Mall. In fact, virtually all Malls have early morning walking programs and they generally do not cost a cent. The YMCA also has great programs for seniors. As do most community Senior centers. Your TV will also surprise you with the number of exercise programs that can be followed in the privacy of your home. There are also many CD's that you can purchase which provide programs you can use at home. Finally, many Health clubs today offer senior programs that you may wish to examine.

You must also be aware of the potential danger of any Hospital or Nursing Home stays. It is very important that anybody who is admitted to one of these facilities have a relative or friend be with them as much as possible to insure that proper care is given.

We must also consider the health of our minds. It is a well known fact that the aging process brings with it the terrible prospect of memory loss, dementia and Alzheimer' disease. While there is much progress being made in these areas, there is still a way to go before these problems are brought under control. However, you must be aware that you can take steps to combat all of these things by following these simple steps.

First, read as much as you can. Go to the Library and spend some time there finding books which will entertain you or educate you.

Second, play mind games with either your spouse or some friends. You will find that they challenge you and make your mind work a bit.

Third, learn to use the computer. There are now available many sites on the internet that allow you to participate in brain enhancing exercises. This will open endless possibilities for you to expand your brain while having some fun.

Fourth, consider taking a course at your local college. Generally, these institutions have special programs for seniors who can attend classes at little or no charge.

Keeping active will stimulate your body and your mind.

Your health is your treasure and you owe it to yourself and your loved ones to plan for your Good Health during the retirement years.

REMEMBER, IT IS NEVER TO LATE, NOR TO EARLY, TO START THE PLANN ING PROCESS!

"'Mid pleasures and palaces though we may roam, be it ever so humble, there is no place like home"

J. Howard Payne

1791-1852

HOUSING

Now we have arrived at one of the more critical questions that will face us in retirement. Where am I going to live and will that be the place, where I will spend the remainder of my life?

For many this question was already answered by simply making a decision that they would stay in their existing home and by others who have already selected a new home in a milder climate or one that is closer to children.

In fact, an AARP study in 2003, found that 80% of persons over the age of 45 stated that they would prefer to stay in their own homes. This is perfectly understandable and at first glance, it seems a very reasonable solution. However, such decisions are generally made for one or more of the following reasons.

1. Familiarity with the area. Nothing feels more comforting than the old familiar places. You grew up there, went to school there, worked there and probably have met, courted and married a spouse there.

2. Family is around you. What is better than having the kids and grandchildren nearby?

3. Friends you know are all around you. Chances are that most of your school friends and fellow workers are still in the area.

4. Financial. You frankly cannot afford to go anywhere else. Real Estate is depressed and you will not generate the money you once thought would be gained when your house was sold.

For whatever combination of reasons you make this decision, remember that Life Comes At You Fast! Suddenly the kids are transferred or simply move to another area. Your friends decide to seek the sun, follow their kids or unfortunately pass away. Your house starts to become a big burden, needs extensive repairs and taxes mount tremendously. Then sadly, the thing you dreaded most occurs and one of the spouses passes away.

My point here is do you have a Plan B in place for such events? What are your options? No problem you say! The kids will take care of us. The reality here is that this will only occur if they are able to take care of you and you wish them to do so. In many situations, there are very legitimate reasons why they cannot help. You must face this fact and be prepared to seek other alternatives. Let us discuss some of these.

1. Senior Lifestyle Communities

Generally referred to as "Over 55 Communities" these have popped up all over the country. Initially these communities were located in the so-called Sun Belt areas. Now however they have started to grow in virtually all areas of the country. They provide a very attractive option for independent retirement living. The main attractions of these communities are freedom from caring for the outside of a home, ability to live in and among other seniors and usually a variety of group activities in which you can participate in. Studies have shown that while their numbers are growing, still only 3 to 4% of retirees are moving into these communities. I suspect that in future years this number will steadily grow.

2. Assisted Living Communities

This type of living arrangement is designed for seniors who have suffered the loss of two or more Activities of Daily Living. These activities are Mobility, Housekeeping, Bathing & Dressing, Toileting, Feeding self, Taking Medication, Mental status and Behavioral status. The Assisted Living facility provides round the clock assistance with such things as medication dispensing, meals, activities and recreation and other life functions. These communities are generally very attractive and provide peace of mind for the senior as well as their family. Many of these newer Assisted Living facilities are sponsored by and affiliated with different Religious sects who make them very attractive to many people.

3. Nursing Facility

This type of living alternative will provide seniors who require round the clock care with a worry free environment where their care is assured.

In a growing number of locations, we are seeing the introduction of multiple purpose facilities whereby you may start in the independent living section, move to assisted living and if necessary go on to skilled nursing care.

4. Live With Relative

This option is gaining some momentum, as parents are moving in with the kids. Some families are building or remodeling homes to include a separate apartment for the parents. In many cases, this is happening for economic reasons.

There are many factors to consider as you look into these different and varied options. Cost may be the number one issue but this should not deter you. You will find that the cost of moving into one of these alternative housing options can be more affordable than you might suspect. The key here is to investigate all of your options thoroughly, so that you can make an informed decision.

There are of course other alternatives to solving the housing question. One of these is a shared living agreement where two or more seniors join and share a home. Another option that has gained some popularity is the Reverse Mortgage program where a senior homeowner can draw cash value out of their home without any repayment until the home is sold or the party passes on. Both of these options require serious investigation and should not be undertaken without the advice of a trusted advisor.

The question of where to live is many times a balancing act as seniors weigh their desire to really retire and enjoy themselves against the realty of having to take care of children or another family member. Society has changed dramatically in the last decade as the traditional idea of retirement has given way to the new realities of our modern world.

Only put off until tomorrow what you are willing to die left undone"

Pablo Picasso

1881-1973

LEGAL

This section is very critical and every person should pay attention to the material we discuss. Many people consider the legal aspect of their lives with little regard. However, believe me when I tell you that a few steps taken early on in your life will give you and your loved ones much peace and comfort.

One of the most important things you will wish to keep in mind is the following; in the absence of a variety of legal documents you should have in place, when you become incapacitated, ill or pass away, you and/or your assets may fall under the control of a third party. Think about that for a moment and understand the impact of such an occurrence. Also, think about your family; why not make it easy for them in what will certainly be a difficult time.

So let us get started!

WILL - you should have made out a will well before you get to retirement age. With a Last Will & Testament, you direct how, to whom and in what manner your assets are to be distributed after you die. It also enables you to name an executor of your estate. This is a very simple thing to accomplish and the benefit of a will is incalculable. Aside from the obvious issue of stating who gets what, the will also can set out guidelines for care of minor children or a disabled child or relative.

We all know of many instances where a senior has failed to leave a will and the resulting fights and controversy among relatives has been sad. Although not everybody may be happy with your will, they will at the very least know exactly where they stand. You must remember that in the absence of a will your assets will fall under the control of the Probate Court when you pass away. Probate is the court-supervised administration of a deceased's estate. If there is no will, the disposition of property is dictated by state intestacy laws. This can be a lengthy and expensive proposition.

POWER OF ATTORNEY - this document will allow you to name a trusted party to administer your affairs should you become ill or disabled. This means that you will have designated a trusted party to pay your bills, manage your money and generally insure that your affairs will be managed properly.

LIVING WILL/HEALTH CARE PROXY - these documents will be critical should you become terminally ill or mentally incapacitated. This will give a trusted party the ability to decide on your behalf what type of medical care and end of life decisions might be made on your behalf. This will insure that your wishes will be carried out and will ease the burden family might have.

BENEFICIARY - you must take care to name a beneficiary (s) for your assets. This will insure they pass directly upon your death in accordance with your wishes.

Be certain your beneficiary designation is always current. Also, be very specific as to how you may wish to have assets pass should there be a break in the beneficiary chain such as a death or divorce, etc.

After you have completed these documents, be certain they are in a safe place. Also, insure that somebody knows where they are located. If you have a safe deposit box, make known the location of the key. Depending on your own personal circumstances, you may wish to have one of your children as a co-signer for a safe deposit box so that they may access it in an emergency.

I cannot stress the importance of having these matters in place. We are not talking about a major expense, as you should be able to get all of this done at relatively little cost. The benefits of being prepared legally are beyond measure and will give you peace of Mind!

"*Dying is a wild night and a new road*"

Emily Dickenson

1830-1886

FINAL WISHES

The biggest favor you can do for yourself, your children and relatives is to plan for your passing in the form of a Final Wishes Statement. We all have experienced the arguments, bitterness and general disruption that arises when one passes away. Needless to say, it is a very difficult and sad time and to have it further disrupted by controversy is a bitter pill to swallow. You can avoid most of this by simply planning for what has to happen to all of us.

BURIAL ARRANGEMENTS - Save everybody a lot of trouble by arranging for the details of your burial. If possible, prepay for the funeral and have a burial plot already purchased. In the case of children, this will relieve them of a great burden.

State exactly how you wish to be dressed. Leave a clear outline of the type of service you wish. Let everyone know beforehand how long you wish to be viewed if at all. Indicate which church you wish to use. Leave instructions for the music to be played and method of your final burial. (Earth, Mausoleum, Cremation)

OBITUARY - It is a very good idea to draft an obituary for yourself. Who knows or remembers how you would like to be remembered better than you? When it is all over, do you want a post funeral gathering?

PERSONAL EFFECTS - save everybody the drama of deciding who will get your personal things. Make a list of your valuable items and place a name next to each item so there will be no misunderstanding of what goes where! Be generous but fair so there will be no animosity after you have left the scene.

PEOPLE TO NOTIFY - leave a detailed list of the persons you wish to have notified of your passing. The list should have their name, telephone number and relationship. This will be most appreciated by all concerned.

LOCATION OF IMPORTANT PAPERS - please, please leave a list of where things can be found. Do not make your kids or other relatives go crazy trying to locate your will, burial papers, financial records and other important data. You may remember that old insurance policy taken out 50 years ago but believe me the kids will know nothing about it. The same with stock certificates and bonds you may have tucked away years ago. Do not risk the possibility of any of these important items being lost forever.

One way you can accomplish all of this is to create a binder or a file that will contain all of these documents and instructions.

One final thing you may wish to consider is to talk these matters over with the children or relatives. Do not make the process a big secret as that will not be in anybody's best interest.

"Work banishes these three great evils, boredom, vice and poverty"

Voltaire

1649-1778

WORK

In the "old days" when one retired, that was it! You walked out of the workplace and never looked back. After all, this was your time and you had earned it. However, in recent years this has changed dramatically. No longer is retirement the long awaited permanent vacation longed for by all. For many reasons the reality of retirement has been altered significantly.

Perhaps the single biggest change has occurred due to the economy and the havoc it has caused among retirees. The biggest culprit in this regard has been the lack of planning on the part of most people. Things were put off in favor of more perceived pressing concerns and the attitude was, retirement is still many years away; I will still have plenty of time to take care of that. Unfortunately, this along with severe blows to personal wealth due to the economy has left many retirees short of the goals they need to remain financially healthy. Therefore, the alternative has been, go back to work! I am certain that many of you have relatives, friends and neighbors who have returned to the workplace. One only needs to observe the employees of most retail stores and you will quickly see the increasing numbers of retirees returning to work.

Some studies have revealed that a significant number of people planning for retirement believe that they will continue working in some capacity after retirement.

Unfortunately, the economic reality of today's world is that your Social Security check just will not cut it any longer. Couple that with the loss of value in savings and many retirees have a dilemma on their hands. You still may be one of the lucky few who have a pension plan but as I have previously mentioned, these plans have been rapidly disappearing. The 401K Plans that in most cases have replaced pension programs are terrific vehicles to set aside funds for retirement but in recent years, concerns have surfaced with these plans. First, it has been noted that individuals are not funding such plans to the degree they should meaning that their plans would possibly fall short of their goal. Secondly, a disturbing trend is emerging where individuals are withdrawing money from plans before retirement. Thirdly, retirees are withdrawing money from their plans ahead of schedule to simply get by.

Remember this critical fact, we are living longer which means that our financial planning must take a longer-term view.

So you decide you must return to work, what do you do? One of the first things you may wish to look into is contacting your old employer. Remember, you have a wealth of knowledge which we refer to as "Institutional Knowledge" that can be very valuable to an employer.

Often times an employer will hire back retired employees as an alternative to hiring and training new people. This can be beneficial to the employer because a rehired retired person is a cheaper investment than a new person is and will generally be more productive in a shorter period. Another benefit to the employer is that a rehired retiree can become a valuable training tool for new employees.

Another route to follow is to contact Non-Profit organizations in your area. Retirees are a terrific source of talent for these groups and they benefit greatly from the expertise you can bring to their table. In my own case, after retirement, I returned to the workforce as a manager for a non-profit organization and enjoyed a number of fulfilling years.

Perhaps you cannot find a full time job, or maybe you just need a part time situation, then you have other routes to explore. Some of these might be:

School District - these employ many people to fill jobs such as classroom aids, bus monitors, library aids, and lunchroom help.

Funeral Directors - most of these employ men part time to act as Pall Bearers, greeters, parking attendants and drivers.

Lawn Care - Especially during the spring and summer, many people are hired to perform general outside lawn and property care tasks.

Messengers - many hospitals, senior centers, banks and drug stores hire people to perform general messenger duties.

These are just a few examples of things you can look into in order to find some part time employment. Always use your imagination and I am certain that many will come up with other ideas in their own environment where they can find a job.

Another source of finding employers who have a record of hiring seniors is AARP. Through their website, you can access a list of potential employers.

Of course, there is also the option of starting a business. Some may wish to explore this route but be warned it is a steep financial slope to navigate and you better be prepared for a lot of work, problems and heartache. This is not a route to follow for the timid!

Whether you return to work due to economic concerns or simply because you are bored, plan your new experience well and do not undertake anything that will create a burden for you.

Volunteering can be an exciting, growing, enjoyable experience. It is truly gratifying to serve a cause, practice one's ideals, work with people, solve problems, see benefits and know one has a hand in this".

Harriet Nagler

VOLUNTEERING

One of the most fulfilling things you can consider doing during retirement is to volunteer. Generally speaking, if you do not need to work, care for grandchildren, have any other personal obligation and enjoy relatively good health, volunteering may be for you! A great satisfaction can be derived from offering your time and talent to help others. The ways in which you can volunteer and the opportunities to do so are limitless. In most cases, you need not possess any special talent but merely need to make yourself available. Your time is your contribution!

In studies conducted on the subject it has been discovered that volunteering can provide many tangible benefits to the individual. Perhaps one of the biggest benefits to be derived from volunteering is the opportunity to fill the void created when you left full time work. You must remember that your work provided you with a stable platform in life. Now there is a gap and you can compensate for the gap by volunteering. Another benefit to be gained from volunteering is the socialization aspect. Having lost the social network of work, you now have the opportunity to meet new people and create new social alliances. A third benefit is the opportunity to make a difference in your community and this can be very rewarding.

As you examine the many volunteer opportunities that may be available, you will find that they range from very simple tasks to situations that are more complex. Therefore, you must be careful to choose your opportunity carefully and be certain that you have a compatible match with your interests and skills. I am certain that when you do volunteer you will come away from the opportunity feeling very good about having contributing to something very worthy.

The opportunities to volunteer are considerable and they range from very simple to more complex situations. Remember that no matter at what level you choose to volunteer, your contribution will be welcome and valuable.

I will attempt to share some Volunteer ideas for you to consider.

<u>Your Church</u> - religious education, decorations, children's programs

<u>American Red Cross</u> - answer phones, blood drives, emergency service

<u>Library</u> - stack shelves, mend books

<u>Senior Center</u>- instruct classes, serve food

<u>Literacy Program</u> - read to children, teach English as second language

<u>Museum</u> - guide, gift shop

<u>Theater</u> - usher, telemarketing

<u>Hospital</u> - gift shop, magazine distribution, transport patients

<u>Hospice</u> - companion, reader

<u>Historical Society</u> - guide, greeter

<u>Veterans Hospital</u> - companion, read to patients, transport

<u>Volunteer Home Care</u> - companion, shopping, errands

<u>Women in Crisis</u> - counselor, reception

<u>United Way</u> - fund drive, telephone work

<u>Food Bank</u> - distribute food, stack pantry

<u>Homeless Shelter</u> - serve meals, reception

<u>Salvation Army</u> - fund raising, sort clothing, disaster assistance

<u>AARP</u> - Tax assistance

In addition, many Support Groups need help.

AA
American Cancer Society
Humane Society
Big Brothers/Big Sisters

By no means, do the groups listed above constitute all of the available opportunities but they are shown to give you an idea of the wide range of situations that do need help.

You may also know of some group or institution that needs some help and you could be instrumental in forming a volunteer group of your own. What a wonderful thought!

Should you wish to get involved in a more intense way there are even more opportunities you might look into. For example if you have business skills, you might consider the Service Corps of Retired Executives commonly known as SCORE.

This would permit you to interact with people starting a business or looking to improve how they operate a business.

For the outdoor minded there are numerous opportunities available in the National Park system as well as in local and state parks. In fact, the National Park Service estimates that 50% of their volunteers are retirees.

Another very worthwhile volunteer opportunity might be found with your local agency that works with the disabled. This can be a most rewarding endeavor for the volunteer.

You will find that the act of volunteering will provide you with much personal reward that comes from helping others.

"Truly nothing is to be expected but the unexpected".

Alice Jane

1876-1916

SAFETY and SECURITY

In my experience, I have found that most people do not tend to pay much attention to this subject. When I find myself in conversation regarding the issues of personal safety people generally treat the subject very lightly. Bear in mind that while covering this topic I cover all aspects of safety ranging from accidents, criminal activity, driving and elder abuse. There are many concerns seniors should be aware of and steps they may consider to assist them in this regard.

According to the Center for Disease Control and Prevention, following are some facts you should be aware of.

1. One out of three adults age 65 and older falls each year.

2. In 2009, 2.2 million nonfatal fall injuries among older adults were treated in emergency departments and more than 581,000 of these were hospitalized.

3. In 2007, 81% of fall deaths were among people 65 and older.

4. The chances of falling and being seriously injured in a fall increase with age.

In 2009, the rate of fall injuries for adults 85 and older was almost four times that for adults 65 to 74.

These are serious facts and older persons can take steps to protect themselves and lessen the chance of such injuries occurring. Here are a few simple things you can do to help yourself.

1. Grab Bars - Install grab bars in bathrooms in and around the tub, shower enclosure, and toilets.

2. Rails - Install hand rails on both sides of stairs.

3. Rugs - Make certain that rugs, which may slide, are removed and replaced with non-stick type rugs.

4. Cords - Be certain that extension cords, lamp and appliance cords are secure and not in the way of where you walk.

5. Heights - Be certain that you do not climb stools, ladders chairs of anything else to get at items in upper shelves and cabinets. Store things you use at lower levels. Obtain an extender that you can use to retrieve items from cabinets.

6. Lighting - Be certain that you have adequate lighting in your surroundings at night. It is an extremely good idea to have a flashlight or other type of light available in each room and in hallways.

Do not rely on your old sense of direction and familiarity with your surroundings to keep you safe! Also, be certain that you have adequate lighting on the outside of your home. This is important!

7. Night Lights - I include this as a separate point as I consider this to be one of the most important things you can do for yourself. You should be certain that all walkways, bathrooms and areas at the top and bottom of steps have a night light! These are very inexpensive devices for you to purchase and they could be a life saver!

Now let's talk about fire safety. Fires are devastating but there are steps you can take to provide some protection.

1. Fire and Smoke Detectors - Your living quarters should have an adequate number of detectors installed at appropriate locations. Newer homes have them in virtually every room. They are inexpensive to purchase but invaluable as a life saving tool. Generally speaking, your local Fire Department or Municipal Building Inspector will readily give you advice in this matter.

2. Escape Plan - Develop a plan as to how you would escape from a fire. If you are disabled, or have a spouse or child who may be disabled, have signs posted for authorities so they can rapidly assist you.

3. Carbon Monoxide - You should have carbon monoxide detectors installed in your living quarters. Again, they are relatively inexpensive but a great defense against what is known as the "silent killer"!

4. In Terms of overall personal safety, you may want to consider having a security alarm installed in your home. This may or may not be within your economic means but is an item that should at least be explored.

In all of the areas I have noted above, you should consult with a trusted advisor or professional who can guide you in making the proper decisions relative to these items.

Your safety against criminal activity is another issue that should be addressed by senior citizens. As you grow older, there are many dangers that you must pay attention to in order to protect yourself. These break down into three general categories:

1. Physical attacks - These include incidents such as home break in, purse snatching and assault. While it is a fact that in general violent crime against seniors is somewhat lower than against the younger population, some types of crimes are actually higher. For example, the FBI in January 2005 issued its report, "Crimes Against Persons Age 65 or Older, 1993-2002" in which they found that seniors generally experienced victimizations at much lower rates than younger groups of people.

There were, however, several categories where seniors did in fact have similar experience. These included Purse snatching/pocket picking and wallet theft. As you can imagine, seniors are ripe targets for these types of crime, as they tend to be more forgetful, less vigilant and easier targets for thieves.

Therefore, it is in your best interest to always safeguard your personal items when shopping and traveling.

Take simple steps such as: Do not expose cash or credit cards. Do not leave your purse or wallet exposed on a counter. Do not leave your purse unattended in a shopping cart or in your car! Simple steps but ones that could save you a lot of grief.

2. Home Break In - Always be certain that you take simple steps to protect your property. These might include such things as insuring that your home has proper locks including dead bolts and door chains. Be certain that windows are also locked and that there is adequate lighting both inside and outside the home.

3. Identity Theft/Scams - There is a growing trend in this area as unscrupulous individuals increasingly prey on seniors. They have targeted this part of the population because they see seniors as vulnerable marks! You should always be cautious whenever somebody presents you with a get rich scheme, home repair or lottery-winning proposition. Any activity of this type should promptly be reported to your local law enforcement.

A key step you might take to further protect yourself against identity theft is to stop putting your outgoing mail in your mailbox. There is a growing trend among thieves to empty the contents of mailboxes in order to gather personal information. The minor inconvenience of mailing directly at the Post Office or giving directly to your carrier can more than offset the trouble you will encounter if your identity is compromised.

In addition, one final thought regarding protection of your identity and personal records. Think very seriously about obtaining a crosscut shredder, as this will insure that unneeded records will be permanently destroyed. These are relatively inexpensive, easy to use and are worth their weight in gold!

Another area that should be highlighted is Elder Abuse. With the growing number of senior citizens who are either under the care of a relative or caregiver in their own home, coupled with those who are in institutional care, instances of abuse are growing. Abuse of the elderly falls into five general categories: physical abuse, sexual abuse, psychological abuse, financial abuse and neglect. While there is no actual data it has been estimated that perhaps as many as 3 to 4% of the elderly suffer some form of abuse. We know that throughout history the weak and vulnerable have been abused by the strong and those in power or in control. If you ever feel that you have been abused in any way, immediately advise a family member, some responsible party or the authorities.

By no means have I touched on every possible topic that involves your safety and security, but my intention is simply to make you aware and hopefully more educated.

"The Family is one of Natures' masterpieces".

George Sentayana

1863-1952

FAMILY AND FRIENDS

How often have we heard or even commented ourselves that you cannot live with them and you cannot live without them! They are our best friends, worst critics, confidants and generally, they are always there for us.

As you enter into your retirement years, you will come to find that their presence in your life will take on even more and newer importance. Thinking back to your work life, you will remember that you most often had a built in support system through your job, professional associations and all kinds of company activity. Truly, you always had family and friends but your life probably centered mostly on your job.

Now that you have retired, you will quickly learn that such support systems will fade away. To be certain there will be the obligatory "we will keep in touch" and "let's get together" but the reality of life is that more often than not the old relationships grow dim and distant. As you examine what happens, you find that it is not so much that people have not been well intentioned but rather their interests and the demands of their lives have changed.

Therefore, it is very important to step back and see what can be done to create a new support system in place of what took place in the past.

Your family has and will always be an important and significant part of your life. I do not mean to suggest that when you had a career they did not figure as much as they might now but facing facts, we all most likely spent much more of our time and energy working hard somewhat at the expense of the family. This is meant as a broad generalization and may not specifically apply to you. However, now the time has come where work is behind you and you can at last redirect attention to family. The children have all grown and are launched in their own careers and families. Perhaps there are grandchildren on the scene. At this point in your life, you can now give them something of immense value. What could that be?

You and your life experience, your attention, your advice and counseling, and most important your presence. Sadly, in growing numbers children today may also need your help. As mentioned earlier this is one of the areas where retirement today has changed.

Conversely you will soon learn that you also will become more dependent on the children. As each year goes by that unbending villain time takes its constant toll on our bodies and our mind.

Then there are your other relatives. Might be brothers and sisters, aunts and uncles or cousins. Some of them may be closer than others but in many cases, they will be sharing the senior years with you.

Now I recognize that in many instances there could be strained family relations. Might be the children or the relatives and often the thing that may have caused the strain has long been forgotten or become obscured with the passing of time. It is at this point in our lives that we must take a hard look in the mirror of life and decide if it will be worth it in the end to continue living in a strained environment. Remember that we only pass this way once and so often there is no second chance to set things right. Carrying on any type of ill will or bad feeling in your senior years is sad and self-destructive. Frankly, I think you would find that there is negative effect on health to live on in this kind of environment.

So why not embrace your family and engage in shared experiences such as: dinners, family game nights, outings, shared social events, shared vacations and other types of activities.

How about your friends? Many of them have been in your life almost as long as some family members. You played with them as children, went through school with them and perhaps even served our country with them. For the most part, they were always there when you needed them. Now in retirement many of them will still be around. True, some have moved on or sadly may be experiencing poor health but still they can play a big part in you senior years. Like family, you can still share many important hours with them and enhance the retirement experience.

Many retirees may choose to move to another part of the country or even to another part of the state. In these cases, it may become necessary to establish new relationships. This might be done simply through a new neighborhood, a new church or even through a senior center. Believe me when I tell you that there are many seniors craving the experience of friendship.

I mentioned earlier that seniors are starting to migrate into the new Adult Living Communities and one of the main drivers of this is the need to form and be in contact with peer groups. Although this is not the answer for all, it may be something for you to consider.

The retirement experience can be the dawn of your new life. The opportunity to share it with family and friends is too big a benefit to ignore.

"A hobby is hard work you wouldn't do for a living".

Anonymous

HOBBIES

One of the most rewarding and self fulfilling endeavors you can undertake is to either grow an existing hobby or start a new one. In my experience, I have found that many seniors no longer engage in any type of hobby. You will find that having a hobby is fun, challenging and keeps your mind in action. All of these are important factors in the senior years.

It could be that you have maintained a hobby for many years and retirement now gives you the opportunity to allocate more of your time and effort to such activity. On the other hand, you may not have had an interest in such an undertaking for a variety of reasons but now in retirement you have the perfect setting to either restart one or begin a new chapter in your life.

Where to start may be your first question but that can easily be answered by examining your interests. I myself engaged in three hobbies during my work career and then into retirement. My first hobby was model railroading. I selected HO gauge trains and started some 30 years ago with one set, which I received as a gift. Somehow, these little trains captured my imagination and throughout those 30 years provided me with countless hours of enjoyment. The one set grew into over 100 pieces of rolling stock and countless buildings and accessories. My second hobby started about 25 years ago when I began to collect Pins. I collected the tie tack type pins from travels and events around the world.

This endeavor yielded me over 1000 pins that I now proudly display on several large boards. Today I have discontinued the trains; maintain the pins and added writing as a third endeavor.

Hobbies provide you with other benefits as you can network with others who share your interest thus establishing a new social network. They also keep your mind active as you engage in investigation and expansion of the hobby.

If you have not enjoyed a hobby in the past, you might wonder where to start. Frankly, it is very easy to launch a hobby. The obvious first step might be to identify one or more things that you enjoy doing and that bring you pleasure. Let us say for example that you have a skill with wood. This can easily be turned into a hobby of making birdhouses, mailboxes or even children's toys. Then there is always the art of coin and stamp collecting. These two endeavors can bring countless hours of enjoyment.

A very interesting activity to engage in during retirement is researching and establishing a family history or family tree. This can be most enlightening and can produce an important historical record, which can be passed on to children and relatives. In many cases, this can also produce some unexpected results such as identification of ancestors and relatives previously unknown to you.

Some other hobbies you may look into are Knitting & Crochet, Gardening, Photography, Restore Furniture, Collectables and Painting. There are so many more things but these are listed to simply give you some ideas. Hobbies can also translate into volunteer opportunities as follows:

Knitting and crocheting for cancer patients, premature babies, shawls for older institutionalized patients.

As you pursue a hobby, it may also be feasible to turn it into a small income producer. Many people have done quite well buying and selling on the internet. Recognizing that often your finances may be stretched I do not want to suggest that large sums of money are required to engage in a hobby. You can do quite well with minimum amounts of money.

Another area you can pursue that may interest you is in learning about the computer. You may not believe that you have the capability or skill to master the computer but take my word for it you can. Many senior centers, local schools and Universities have programs available to seniors specifically for the purpose of learning these skills. The same holds true for many of the hobbies listed before.

The real point to this entire subject is to provide more ways for you to enjoy retirement, utilize your time and keep your brain and body active. The rewards in doing this are great and the personal satisfaction will make you feel revitalized!

"My favorite thing is to go where I've never been".

Diane Arbus

1924-1971

TRAVEL

The dream of every retiree is to travel. "I am going to see the world", is the refrain echoed by all! Normally I would say that everybody should hit the road but the reality of today's world places some limits on our ability to get out and get going. Limited finances, high gas prices and a variety of other issues have put somewhat of a damper on the ability of many to travel.

However, you can still scratch the travel itch if even in a reduced manner. Travel need not always involve some foreign destination or even a cruise but can be more modest. Most senior centers have very active schedules for trips that vary from same day to a week or more. In many instances, they offer rates that can be more affordable. In addition, more importantly, they offer the opportunity to take these trips with friends. You may also do the same thing through church groups or your local place of worship.

Of course, there is always the ability to take your own day trip. Why not gather a couple of friends and share the travel cost to visit a museum, seaport, exhibition, show, etc. This makes more trips feasible and generally allows you more flexibility in getting away.

As far as a cruise or foreign trip is concerned, you should be on the lookout for deals that are constantly offered. Quite often, you will see advertisements for Buy one, Second goes free.

Stay two nights, get a third night free. These types of deals can allow you to make a trip that you thought might be impossible to enjoy.

Whenever you travel whether it is for the day or longer, always watch for and ask for senior discounts. Virtually everybody offers some sort of deal for you. Remember that if you belong to a club, credit union or have certain credit cards, there may be discounts associated with that membership or card.

Another travel tip, which you might find interesting, is to take a trip with Road Scholar, formerly known as Elderhostel. The stated mission of Road Scholar is, "empower adults to explore the world's places, peoples, cultures and ideas". They offer a wide variety of trips and make them available at reasonable cost. Another big advantage of this program is that you travel with and enjoy other retirees who share similar interests.

You may also use travel as a vehicle to explore and examine potential places to either retire to or for vacation.

If travel is in your plans here are some valuable tips you may wish to remember.

1. Insurance - whenever possible obtain trip insurance. It is relatively inexpensive and can benefit you greatly should you have to cancel a trip due to illness or some other emergency.

2. Medical - If you have a health concern, you may wish to check out the availability of travel medical insurance. Remember that Medicare will not be accepted in foreign countries so it might be advisable to have some alternative plans.

Although your retirement travel plans may not be the same as your dreams, they still can be fun and enjoyable and will provide you with much pleasure.

"Today is the first day of the rest of your life".

Charles Dederich

1913-1997

FIRST DAYS

The day has finally arrived, the first day of retirement! You may think that you have all of the answers about retirement and are primed to step out of your job on Friday and start retirement on Monday without missing a beat, but you may be in for a few surprises. Remember that you have had no special training for this moment nor was there any instructional booklet for you to read.

The first feeling you may have is a new sense of freedom. Gone are schedules, alarm clocks and any sense of urgency to be anywhere. When this new feeling begins to sink in you will begin to appreciate your new station in life.

Closely following the freedom, you may begin to experience a sense of loss. I know, I have heard it a hundred times from countless retirees. It goes like this, "I am going to walk out that door at work and never look back"! Yes, there are a few who manage to accomplish this but for most what happens is there is now a void in their life. Think about this for a moment. The average worker has spent approximately 44 years working. Basically that means that you went somewhere every day for those 44 years and had each day filled with work, responsibility, friends and a work social circle. Suddenly that has all disappeared! This is a big gap to fill!

Next you may find that the people in your personal life are not prepared to have you around 24/7. Your retirement in effect interrupts the lives of others who will not experience any profound change in their daily schedules. Now they have to figure out how their schedule will change in order to accommodate you.

The good news is that all of this change does begin to fall in place given a little time. Lifestyles gradually adapt and you and everybody else will eventually adapt to the new lifestyle.

In the early stages of retirement, most people seem to maintain their same level of energy, the same outlook on life, the same interests and in general life moves on but at a more leisurely pace. The real changes begin to happen in the subsequent years and at first they manifest themselves in subtle ways. I would like to review some of these now.

Your Mind will begin to slow down and you will experience the gradual decline of your memory and cognitive powers. This is a very natural part of the aging process and for the majority of seniors this does not limit them in any significant way. In others, this decline may lead to life altering illness. For this reason, it is essential that you engage in and utilize the many tools available to maintain your mental capacity.

Your vision may also suffer somewhat but this can be corrected by proper eye care and diet.

Your hearing will probably begin to decline somewhat. Current data suggests that in the over 65 age group some hearing loss is experienced by 30% of seniors and that percentage can escalate in the later years.

Your bones and joints will certainly suffer some deterioration simply due to the aging process. Again, you will find that proper diet and exercise can slow down this process in the body.

In virtually all of the above noted areas of concern modern medical care and research has slowed down these problems considerably and as a result, retirement lifestyle is improving.

Other things that will start to emerge in the retirement year's deal with how the general population reacts to and treats seniors. You often wonder why people do not stop for a moment and think, "That will be me one day".

For example, when you are driving you will start to become more cautious and that in turn will annoy other drivers. Given the lack of patience and respect in the general populace, this will reflect in them expressing some degree of anger, as you will be perceived as slowing them down.

If you happen to do some grocery shopping you will find it harder to reach many items as stores do not seem to recognize the limitations of seniors and continue to stack shelves high and deep.

The frustration of this is that they do not seem to do anything to alleviate the situation.

It is not all bad news, as you will find many benefits become available to retirees. Some of these are reduced price tickets for movies, free admission to state parks, discount days at some supermarkets, reduced prices on meals, etc.

You will find that there are many resources available to you and they can provide you with a wealth of information on virtually any subject you might find useful. If you have access to and are comfortable on the computer, most of these resources are simple to access. If not you can always call or write and obtain the same information but it will take you a bit longer to obtain it. At the rear of this book I have included a list of some valuable resources which you will find helpful.

THERE IS NO QUESTION THAT LIFE IN RETIREMENT WILL CHANGE, BUT, IF YOU ARE FOREWARNED AND HAVE PLANNED WELL, THESE CHANGES WILL NOT STAND IN THE WAY OF A COMFORTABLE AND REWARDING RETIREMENT!

CONCLUSION

Life used to be so simple and uncomplicated! But today we all know that life as we knew it has changed. Who would ever have imagined that our world, our society, our families, our health and our finances would change so dramatically and in effect alter the world of Retirement?

I worry that so many are unprepared for their Retirement. I also know that for those who are serious in their pursuit of a Happy Retirement the tools are out there for them to use. All that is required is a mindset that will encourage you to start planning as soon as possible for this event.

YOU CAN DO IT!

RESOURCE GUIDE

Over the years and while I was researching this book I have learned that there are many resources available to older Americans. These resources can provide a wealth of information on virtually every aspect of Retirement and Aging, they are easy to access and there is generally no cost associated with obtaining the information you seek. By no means does this list encompass the total universe of resources but, it will certainly give you a great starting point.

SOCIAL SECURITY
U.S. Social Security Administration
Office of Public Inquiry
6401 Security Blvd.
Baltimore, MD 21235
Soc.Sec.gov 1-800-722-1213
(Also your local Office if nearby)

FINANCES
Questions about Pensions
Pension Benefit Guaranty Board (PBGC)
POB 151750
Alexandria, VA 22315-1750
Pbgc.gov   1-800-400-7242

Questions and help for Financial Planning
The National Association of Personal Financial Planners
3250 N. Arlington Heights Rd. - Suite 109
Arlington Heights, IL 60004
Info@Napfa.org   847-483-5400

ORGANIZATIONS FOR OLDER AMERICANS

American Association of Retired Persons
601 E Street NW
Washington, DC 20049
aarp.org   1-800-687-2277

Alliance for Retired Americans
815 16th Street NW - 4th Flr.
Washington, DC 20006
retiredAmericans.org   1-800-333-7212

CREDIT REPORTS

Request annual free credit report.
Annual Credit Report Request Service
POB 105281
Atlanta, GA. 30348-5281
Annualcreditreport.com   1- 877-322-8228

PRESCRIPTION DRUG ASSISTANCE

Partnership for Prescription Assistance
pparx.org   1-888-477-2669

IDENTITY THEFT

To obtain an ID Theft Affidavit
Identity Theft Clearing House, FTC
600 Pennsylvania Av.
Washington, DC 20580
Consumer.gov/idtheft   1-877-438-4338

HEALTH AND RELATED ISSUES ON AGING

National Institute of Health
9000 Rockville Pike
Bethesda, MD 20892
Nihi.gov   301-496-4000

National Institute on Aging
Bldg. 31, Rm 5C27
31 Center Dr. MSC2292
Bethesda, MD 20892
Nia.nih.gov   301-496-1752

TRAVEL
Information & questions about Senior Hostel Travel programs
Road Scholar
11 Avenue deLafayette
Boston, MA 02111
roadscholar.org   1-800-454-5768

REFERENCES

Administration on Aging
U.S. Department of Health & Human Services
"A profile of older Americans: 2009

AARP 2003 These Four Walls
"Americans 45 + talk about home and community"

Centers for Disease Control & Prevention
"Falls among older Adults :An overview"

Employee Benefit Research Institute
"2011 Retirement Confidence survey "

The National Center for Victims of Crime
"Commonwealth of PA -2008"

AP-LifeGoesStrong.com
"Baby Boomers Retirement Survey - 2011"

U.S. Census Bureau
"Projections of population by age groups"

U.S. Department of Justice - Office of Justice Programs
"Crimes against persons - Age 65 Or older, 1993-2002"

Wells Fargo Bank, NA
"2010 Wells Fargo Retirement Study"